INTERVIEW

Land Your Dream Job

Step by Step Guide Through Interview From Beginning to The End

by

Tom Mahalo

Tom Mahalo

The information provided herein is stated to be truthful and consistent, in that any liability, in terms of inattention or otherwise, by any usage or abuse of any policies, processes, or directions contained within is the solitary and utter responsibility of the recipient reader. Under no circumstances will any legal responsibility or blame be held against the publisher for any reparation, damages, or monetary loss due to the information herein, either directly or indirectly.

Respective authors own all copyrights not held by the publisher.

The information herein is offered for informational purposes solely, and is universal as so. The presentation of the information is without contract or any type of guarantee assurance.

The trademarks that are used are without any consent, and the publication of the trademark is without permission or backing by the trademark owner. All trademarks and brands within this book are for clarifying purposes only and are the owned by the owners themselves, not affiliated with this document.

Tom Mahalo

Table of Content

Introduction

I want to thank you and congratulate you for getting the book, "*INTERVIEW: Land Your Dream Job-Step by Step Guide Through Interview From Beginning to The End*".

This book has actionable information that can help you get through the interview process from the beginning to the end.

Now that you've received the email, call or SMS that has brightened your day after sending your application for a certain vacancy, then what? How do you ensure that you secure the job? How do you ensure that you beat all the other candidates who've also been shortlisted for an interview? Well, these and many other thoughts could overwhelm you in many ways. While you may be excited at the thought that there is a likelihood of you getting the job, part of you is still scared that you might mess it all up. So what should you do about that? Well, this book will help you to understand the interview process.

This guide's main theme is to provide you with tips you can use to ace your job interview and land your dream job. It will cover various aspects such as the preparations you must make prior to the interview, how to sell yourself to your employer, tips on how to answer interview questions, very common interview questions you can expect and tips on how to answer these questions, and many more aspects to help you land your dream job.

It is good to note that an interview is conductible through various mediums such as via Skype, one-on-one, phone, email, etc. Whichever method the interviewer uses, you can employ the tips mentioned in this write-up and excel in your interview.

Are you ready to get started on the journey to your dream job? Well, then, jump to the next section.

Thanks again for downloading this book, I hope you enjoy it!

When an employer needs to fill a position in his or her company, he or she may give out a written test to prospective job applicants, or have the applicants go through several, testing-for-job compatibility steps before acceptance as the ideal candidate. The final stage of the recruitment process is the interview process with the employer. A job interview is viewable from two angles: from the employer's perspective, and from the prospective employee's perspective.

For the employer, a job interview is the final process where he or she gets to meet with prospective employees. It gives the employer an opportunity to assess the employee as a way to ensure he or she is fit for the job.

From the employee's perspective, a job interview serves two purposes; first, it is an opportunity to meet the employer and to sell him/herself to the employer to and land his/her dream job.

For this write up, we are going to discuss a job interview from an employee's angle.

So how do you prepare for an interview after you've received the call, text, or email notifying you that there will be an interview at a certain time? That's what we will learn in the first chapter.

How to Prepare For a Job Interview

After you get a job interview invitation from a company, you must prepare to enable you pass your interview and land your dream job. This section will discuss some of the preparations you need to make in readiness for your interview.

Research the Company

This is the first step to being ready for your interview. Spend some time trying to learn as much information as possible about your prospective employer as possible. This will show your prospective employer you are not the lazy type because no employer wants to employ a lazy and laid-back employee.

Some information you need to know about the company includes, clear information about the company's background; this may include the time of incorporation. Secondly, you may need to get access to the company's public documents such as Memorandum of Association (MOA) and the company's Articles of Association (AOA). These public documents are easily accessible from the company's corporate office; they give you information about the company's objectives and goals.

The interviewer can chip in one or two questions relating to the company's objectives to see how far you went in your research. In addition, get informed on the trends and news related to the job post, description, and competitors in the field.

Prepare Questions You Will Ask Your Employers

Contrary to popular belief and dogma, an interview should not be one-way. Allowing the interviewer to throw questions at you makes it looks like a one-sided affair. Most employers may mistake it to mean you are not smart or innovative.

To avoid painting a bad picture about yourself, you have to prepare some questions to ask your interviewers. Asking your intended employer. questions makes the interview session active and gives the employer a good impression. You can ask about the interviewer's work background and how long he or she has worked in the company. This type of question will help you bond with the interviewer fast. When there is a bond or understanding between you and the interviewer, he or she will be more thrilled to get you on board the company bus.

You can also ask questions about new markets the company is planning to explore or even the professional growth mechanism the company is employing. Such questions help reflect your need to help the company achieve its future goals.

Other great questions you can ask during an interview session are; whom you will work with, whom you will report to, the entire scope of your job, and the company's expectations (be mindful of how you ask the last two because you do not want to come off uninformed about the job requirements. Remember; it is not what you say but how you say it).

Contact Your References

During the job application stage, there is always a column where you fill your references. You need to contact your references a day or two before the interview to alert them that a prospective employer may call to confirm a few things about you. Most interviewers tend to contact your references immediately after the interview if they feel you are the best candidate for the job; your references being unavailable does not create a good impression.

Prepare For Questions

Questions are inevitable in an interview session. How you tackle and answer your interview questions will determine if you are going to land that position or not. We will discuss in detail common questions to expect during a job interview and how to answer these questions later.

You should expect lots of questions from your interviewer. That's why it will do you good to prepare for these questions well ahead of time. Most of the questions asked during the interview will revolve around your long-term plans, your career goals, your work strengths, past strengths, and weakness.

Examples of questions to expect include:

✓ *What is your biggest weakness?*

✓ *Where do you see yourself career wise in the next 5 to 10 years?*

✓ *Why do you want the job?*

✓ *Why did you leave your last job?*

What you should do before going for a major job interview is to make a list of all probable questions the interviewer may ask. You can do this by asking yourself, "If I were looking for a person to fill this position, which questions would I ask the person, what would I want to know?"

After compiling a list of possible interview questions, go ahead and write down answers to each of the questions. You can do some research online on how to answer specific interview questions then try to write down the modified answers (you will need to modify the answers that you get online to fit the particular job interview). Although you will not provide the answers word for word when the questions come up during an interview, doing this will give you an idea of expected answers.

Practice with A Friend

The next action you should take before the interview is to spend some time practicing with a good friend. Your friend should act as the interviewer or your potential employer, while you should play the role of the employee (interviewee). This is referred to as a mock interview. It will be more beneficial to you if your friend is in a career similar to the job you are applying for.

The aim here is to get a feel of what to expect during the interview. Since you need this job (you would not be going for the interview if it were otherwise), do not water down it importance. Therefore, call two or three friends a few days before the interview then ask them to be the interviewers (you can have them form an interview panel) while you act as the interviewee. Your friends should ask you all the possible questions you have written down beforehand, while you should aim to answer them as though you are facing a real interview panel.

At the end of, have your friends review your performance on a scale of 1 to 10, and point out the areas you need to make improvements on. Repeat the procedure again before the actual day of the interview.

Note: There is power in preparation. While nothing might really prepare you adequately for the real thing, the truth is that you will feel less anxious when you have a mock interview as compared to when you just show up at the real interview with zero preparation. It is just like preparing for an examination- the more you prepare for it, the more confident you feel when you sit for the exam. The opposite is true!

Confirm Time of Interview

Go through your interview invitation letter, email or SMS, or call the company before the actual date of the interview to confirm the actual date and time of the interview. After confirming the date and time, slot it into your schedule lest you forget. Include the interview in your future To-do list on your phone and computer and set it on calendly.com so you can receive an email notification a day before the interview.

That is it for the preparations you need to make before the interview. In the next section, we shall look at how to prepare on the day of the interview.

Day of Interview: How to Prepare

On the day of the interview, some actions you take can reduce tension through the day and help you ace the interview. Some of the actions are in your normal daily routine while the others are unique activities aimed at helping you reduce tension. In this section, we shall discuss what it is you should do on the day of the interview to maximize your chances of impressing the interviewers and landing a job.

Wake up Early

Ensure you wake up early on the day of the interview. You may need to go to sleep early on the night before to make sure you wake up early. Waking up early will give you ample time to make your final preparations and get to your interview venue on time. Setting an alarm clock will help you wake up early.

"How early should I wake up you may ask?" How early you wake will depend on various factors such as the time of the interview and other activities you need to do before you leave for the interview. However, it helps to wake up at least 1 hour earlier than your usual wake up time. Taking a few minutes to meditate and centre yourself when you wake up will help condition your mind for the task ahead.

Mark Out Some Exercise Time

One other activity you need to engage in before you set out for your interview is exercise or engage in any physical activity guaranteed to increase your heartbeat. Exercises, especially aerobatic exercises, aid the release of hormones called endorphins.

Endorphin reduces stress and make you feel good throughout the day. Spend at least 30 minutes exercising before you leave for your interview. Remember that the more strenuous the exercise, the better result you will get.

Note: Engage in physical exercise before leaving from the house for the interview. You don't want to arrive at the interview room all sweaty and panting!

Eat a Healthy Breakfast

Due to the tension of the day's activity, most people prefer not to eat before heading out for an interview. That is wrong. It is best to consume a healthy breakfast before you go for a morning interview. You do not want a situation where you become hungry during, or just before the interview session. Fruits, vegetables, and fibre-rich foods will provide the nutrients you need to get through your day. Go for a balanced diet rich in fibre and a good amount of fruits and proteins

Keep time

One thing you must do on the day of the interview is to ensure you get to the interview venue well ahead of the actual interview time. Reporting late for a job interview creates a very bad impression; that single mistake can make you miss the job opportunity you qualify for and deserve.

To avoid the trouble, be punctual because it will help you complete last minute preparation before going in for the interview. Try as much as you can to get to the interview venue at least 30 minutes before the actual time. Spend the little extra time meditating and engaging in positive self-talks aimed at helping you build up the self-confidence you need to calmly sail through the interview.

Carry an Extra Copy of Your Curriculum Vitae

Just to be on the safe side, it is advisable to carry an extra copy of your CV when reporting for an interview. Although you submitted your C.V during the job application procedure, your interviewer may want to run through some details on your resume with you; you will need a personal copy of your CV for that.

Dress for the Interview

How you dress for an interview matters a lot. There is a popular saying "you are addressed the way you are dressed"; take extra care to ensure you dress to impress your interviewer (s). Remember this is your opportunity to create a good first impression and your dressing will go a long way to help you create a good impression.

Shabby dressing passes the message you are a shabby person and thus your work process and result will be shabby or clumsy: no employer wants that kind of person aboard the workforce bus. Dressing smart on the other hand portrays you as a smart and sharp person capable of completing and acing any task assigned.

How to Dress for an Interview: Invaluable Tips

Are you unsure of what it means to dress well for an interview? The tips below should give you some amazing ideas:

- ✓ **Avoid 'Shouty' Colours:** 'Shouty' colors are bright and noticeable colours. Examples of such colors included, light green, orange, and pink. Imagine wearing an orange suit and a red shirt to an interview; you will look very ridicules and funny. Always go for subdue colors like black, navy blue, and light blue.

- ✓ **Maintain Absolute Neatness:** Look your very best and ensure your clothes are neat, wrinkle free and well ironed. If you can afford a dry cleaner, take the clothes to the dry cleaners. If not, you can do the laundry yourself. The point here is to ensure you look very neat and presentable during the interview.

✓ **Use Very Little Accessories:** Minimize your accessories to the barest minimum. If you are a woman, reduce your make-up to the barest minimum.

Interview Dress Code for Females

If you are a female, the best way to dress for a job interview is to wear a knee length skirt that is not too tight or too bogus- the color should be a dark color preferably black or navy blue. You can pair this with a female shirt, preferably white or blue in color, a pair of black closed-toe shoes, and a blazer or jacket in the same color as your skirt. Apply very little make-up. In addition, limit your accessories to just a ring and your wristwatch.

Interview Dress Code for Males

If you are a male on the other hand, a well-ironed white shirt is ideal. In addition, ensure to wear a dark colored suit, preferably black and a tie. Keep in mind that a bow tie does not look formal for a job interview so you should stick to a tie-the color of the tie should not be too bright; a navy blue or black tie or even a dark striped tie will serve the occasion. The shoe should be a well-polished black show.

These are most of the preparations you need to make on the day of your job interview. In the next session, we will go into the interview and give you tips to help you ace your interview and land your dream job without stress.

Steps-By-Step Guide through a Successful Job Interview

To land your dream job, you need to pass your interview. A successful interview is achievable through good body language, answering all questions with the right answers, and your ability to sell your brand to your interviewers or your employers.

Chances are; you are not the only person invited for the interview. This should not worry you, or cause you to bust into feats of panic attack. Competition is always good; if you ace the interview and land the job despite the presence of other candidates, it means the employer thinks you are ideally suited for the job and are immensely valuable to the company.

If this did not reassure you or make you feel any better about landing your dream job, follow the steps below to make yourself irresistible to your interviewer (s) and land your dream job.

Greet the Panel

As soon as you step into the interview room, the very first thing you have to do is greet the interviewer(s) or panel. Most people create a wrong impression by allowing the interviewer to be the first to greet them at the start of an interview session. Greeting, as minor as it may seem gives the impression that you are homely, accommodating, and not hostile to work with.

A simple 'Good morning Sir' or 'Good afternoon Ma'am' is enough greeting to get the conversion going. A lively smile should accompany the greeting. The smile shows you are confident, not stressed, and prepared for the interview session.

Be Ready To Entertain Questions

After the initial greeting, some interviewers may make small talk or conversations before starting the questions session. The point is; immediately after the greeting, you should be ready to entertain interview/job unrelated questions. How you answer the questions matters a lot. That is why we earlier recommended practicing common interview questions the day before the interview. We shall discuss tips on how to answer interview questions, common interview questions to expect, and how to answer the questions later in this book.

Nevertheless, one thing you should be bear in mind is that answering questions is not an opportunity to start telling your interviewer about your personal and family problems. Questions should be succinct and straight to the point without beating around the bush. In addition, be very honest when answering any of the questions.

Ask Your Own Questions

To avoid making the interview a monotonous session, ask questions during the interview. Asking your own question(s) does not mean you have an opportunity to ask irrelevant or demeaning questions. Your questions must be relevant to the subject of the interview or the future role you will play in the company.

Examples of questions you can ask may be:

- ✓ *The company's plan to outsmart the tough competitor in the market*

- ✓ *If the company allows employees to bring their own ideas on board to help achieve goals faster*

- ✓ *If employees are trusted enough to work with little or no supervision*

You can also ask your interviewer to shed more light on a relevant point he or she mentions during the interview. Avoid asking very personal questions or questions having to do with finances. For example, asking your interviewer how much the company wants to pay you if they employ you will make it look as though you are just there for the money or other benefits. Your interviewers will reveal that information to you at the right time.

Round Up With a Note of Thanks

You will create an impressionable mark on your interviewer (s) if you take a few minutes to thank your interviewer (s) for making out time to be with you. This single act also shows that you have a polite personality. The thank you should come after the whole question and answer session. You can simply say "thank you for creating time from your busy schedule to make this session possible." Or any other thankful remark.

With that in mind, let us take it a step further by outlining tips on how to answer a job interview question.

How to Answer Job Interview Questions

We earlier mentioned that a job interview serves as an avenue for a potential employee to sell him/herself as the best candidate to fill a job position. The best way to achieve this is by minding how you answer questions asked during the interview.

The following tips will serve as a guide to help you answer your interview questions perfectly:

Give Clear and Straight To the Point Answers

When answering interview questions, always ensure your answers are clear. Vague answers will make it seem as though you are trying to hide some details from your interviewer, which will ruin your chances of passing the interview. Try to be as clear and straightforward as possible when you give your answers.

For instance, if an interviewer asks, "why do you want to leave your present position?"Giving an answer like "I am leaving because I am no longer comfortable working there" is a very vague answer that will give off an impression that things are not right in your present work place. But this answer "although I enjoy my present position, I am seeking out another opportunity that will be more challenging as a way to keep up with trends in the industry," is clear and straight to the point.

In addition, do not beat around the bush while giving your answers. Your interviewers do not intend to spend all day interviewing you; therefore, your answers should be short and straight to the point. Avoid using slangs; always maintain a formal language with all your answers.

Avoid Discussing Personal Problems

Your interviewers have no business knowing your personal problems. Mentioning your personal problems during an interview session will put off the interviewer/s, and diminish your chances of landing the job. Stick to discussing career issues and making valid points on why you are the best candidate for the job.

This sort of reply "I nearly finished my MSC program but lost my mother along the line, so I had to drop out. I am also working two jobs to keep my father in an old people's home" is clearly pointing out your personal problems, which is a huge turn off for any employer or interviewer. Your focus should be on selling yourself as the best candidate for the job and not trying to get your interviewer's sympathy.

Body Language Matters

As you speak, give off positive body language or signs. Some positive body language you can show include smiling and maintaining eye contact with your interviewer. You can also use hand gestures when necessary.

Positive body language helps you feel more relaxed and confident. Maintaining eye contacts when speaking does not come naturally to everybody. If it does not come natural to you, you can practice with a friend before the actual day of interview.

Focus On Your Best Attributes

Your answers during a job interview should project your best attributes. You should focus more on your strengths; career highlights and achievements in the field. Some employers may try to break through this format by asking sensitive questions like your greatest weakness.

Even when a potential employer asks such a question, your answer should portray how your strengths triumph over your weaknesses and make them almost invisible. We will talk about how to answer the question about your weakness in the next session.

What you should take away from here is that your answers should focus on the notable achievements you have made in your career, major skills you have picked up that make you stand out from others, and any other positive attributes you have.

Don't Assume Your Interviewer Went Through Your Resume

Some interviewees make the mistake of assuming their interviewer went through their resume before the interview, thus they leave out some vital information during the interview.

Do not make such assumptions because most employers do not make out time to go through all the details of your resume before the interview. Every vital detail that is important to your interview should find mention during the interview even if you stated such details in the resume you submitted.

Do Not Bad Mouth Anybody

Some interviewees make the mistake of bad mouthing or speaking ill about other person(s), in their bid to create an irresistible image to their interviewer. Speaking ill about someone else will definitely not get you the job. No employer wants to have an employee that will go around speaking ill or spreading untrue information about other employees or the company.

Even if you have an issue with your former or present employer, avoid speaking badly about such employer in a job interview because the employer in question may be a friend to your interviewer.

Common Interview Questions and How to Tackle Them

This section will focus on common questions asked in almost every job interview. For each question mentioned, we will discuss the best way to answer the question.

"Introduce Yourself to Us"

This is usually the very first question asked in any job interview. The question can also be phrased in different ways like "Could you tell me a little about yourself, or May I know you?"

Any way the question is phrased, it has the same meaning. What the interviewer or your employer simply wants is for you to give a summary of your career highlight. This question often sets the tone of the conversation that will lead to the interview proper. This is not the appropriate time to tell stories about your life or give off very intimate personal information. Rather, it is an opportunity to introduce your basic personal information as well as emphasize on your career background and stand point.

That does not mean you should take this opportunity to recite all the details of your resume or your curriculum vitae. The question is an indirect request for you to brief your interviewer on your career success and achievements. To answer this question appropriately, try to understand the question from the interviewer's perspective. What is the interviewer trying to know by asking this question?

First, your interviewer sees it as a way to start a conversation that will lead to the proper interview. Secondly, the interviewer wants to find out enough information about your career experience to help him/her decide if you are the best candidate to fill the job position.

Bearing these details in mind, the best way to answer this question is to include details about your career experience, qualifications that match the job description, your career high points and finally, how you relooking for a new challenge and why you feel the job is best for you.

How to Introduce Yourself

1. **Start with Who You Are**: Chances are that your interviewer already knows your name, so you have to skip that aspect and begin with a professional introduction. A good example of a professional introduction is "I am a Computer Programmer with over 6 years of experience creating software in a fortune 100 company."

2. **Highlight Your Skills:** The next step is to highlight some key skills that set you aside from other candidates. For instance, you can say "I have spent the last 6 years as a major developer for ABC company. I have worked with major programming languages such as Python, C#, Ruby, PHP and Java. In fact, I am directly in charge of the team that worked to create XYZ software popularly used for videoing screen cast. Besides working on computer software, I also have experience on mobile application

development both on the IOS and Android platforms."

3. **Mention Why You Are gunning For the New Job:** After providing these highlights, the interviewer will be intrigued to know why you want to leave your current position. It is best to point that during your introduction. You can put it this way "Although I love my current role, I am looking for a more challenging position where I will be able to use more of my potentials."

Note that your introduction should be short and straight to the point. You should not take more than 2 to 4 minutes to complete the introduction.

"What Attracted You to The Company?"

This is where you show your interviewer you did your background research about the company. To answer this question, you need to highlight the company's objectives, culture, or achievements and find a way to link your career goals with the company's objective and goals.

For instance, you can say, "As a Computer Programmer, I have always wanted to work in a company that makes use of a combination of programming languages to produce unique software's and applications. From my little research on the software's and apps created by this company over the years, I deduced that most of these apps were created from a combination of at least two programming languages instead of the conventional use of a singular programming language. Therefore, I think coming on board to work for this company will give me the chance to make use of my knowledge of various programming languages to work on creating unique software for the company."

"What Are Your Greatest Strengths?"

This is an opportunity to make mention of your soft skills which you think the company wants. Remember to mention the skills you are very good at because your interviewer may ask for a demonstration before you are finally given your employment letter. .

"What Is Your Greatest Weakness?"

This is a very tricky question and you have to be very careful with the answer you provide because you can give off a bad impression about your person if you give a negative reply.

The best way to tackle this question is to present your weakness in such a way that it will seem as though your strength can make up for it. On the hand, you can also show that you are making efforts to correct the weakness. For instance, you can say, "My major weakness is time management. However, I am currently taking a time management course to help me tackle this challenge."

"How Do You Handle Stress?"

This can be rephrased as "can you work under stress?" You answer should portray your ability to handle stress well and provide some things you do to help ease and manage work related stress. For instance, you can mention you create a To-do list at the beginning of the day or you ask for a colleague's assistance when the workload exceeds your potential.

"How Much Do You Expect As Salary?"

This is another tricky question. It is advisable not to mention a specific amount unless you have done thorough background research on the company to know they can easily pay the amount you cite. It is much better to ask for a salary range. However, to be on the safe side, it is better to point to the fact that money is not your motivator; rather, you want to advance in your career.

That does it for common questions you can expect from an interview. However, as we indicated earlier, job interview questions will vary depending on the position, company, interviewer, and a range of other factors. It is for this reason why it is important to create a list of all possible questions a day or two before the interview and practice them.

<u>Conclusion</u>

Acing an interview and landing your dream job is not as nerve wrecking as we often make it out to be. By exercising well and exercising good judgment and calmness, your dream job is merely a few questions away. This write-up has equipped you with all the information you need to ace any job interview and land your dream job.

Thank you again for getting this book!

I hope this book was able to help you to understand how you can prepare for an interview, ace it and land your dream job.

The next step is to implement what you have learnt. Good luck and congratulations for landing your new job☺.

Finally, if you enjoyed this book, would you be kind enough to leave a review for this book on Amazon?

I decided to add some value to this book and hopefully help you today. I added new bonus chapter "Starting a business" Enjoy reading!

BONUS - Starting a Business

One of the most challenging aspects of running your own business comes from how you manage the beginning of the business. There are numerous questions that you need to find a genuine answer to, such as;

- *How do you present your business?*
- *How will you market yourself?*
- *What kind of market is there for your business?*
- *Can you get access to products and supplies?*
- *Is there a local demand or do you have to expand?*
- *Will you start as an offline or online business?*
- *Do you need funding to get started?*
- *How much competition do you have?*

With so many questions to consider and not enough time to get all of the answers, you have to consider the best way to move forward from a financial point of view. In this section, starting a Business, we'll take a closer look at the kind of answers that you might be looking for to answer each and every one of these vital questions for business startup.

How do you present your business?

This is how you will try and come across – every business needs to have a set range of parameters that it follows at all times with how it wants to come across. What's the theme? What are you trying to build?

Your business should have some kind of end-game or answer that it provides and speaks to. For example, if you were selling dietary supplements then you would wish to come across with authority and as the solution needed. Your business has to match the kind of attitude your solution provides.

How will you market yourself?

Getting marketing off the ground is perhaps a question for later on in the process but you will find that smart marketing of your business will come from how you try to come across online and/or offline. You have to look at various factors like your target market, how easily you can handle shipping to further locations and how you can get noticed in more than one place.

What kind of market is there for your business?

There are numerous markets open to you in any line of business but each industry is different. Some have different avenues to go down from selling specific products based around that to finding supplemental products and/or services that relate to that service. The market depends on your industry but should be something that you take into full consideration before going any further.

Can you get access to products and supplies?

You'll have to know before you start if you can get access to the products or services needed to make the business work. This might sound obvious, but you would be shocked at how many businesses start up and use the wrong information and don't have the correct details in place long before they get started.

Is there a local demand or do you have to expand?

Take this into account as it might answer the next question, too. If you have a catchment area that is very specific then you might be best served concentrating on offline business methods more. If you have to go a bit further afield to find clients then you might find that going online will be the most effective service for you initially.

Will you start as an offline or online business?

The same as above, but something you should always take into account. Whilst no business should concentrate on just one, you need to have a major preference to be a proper success. This will help you concentrate marketing efforts and help you really see and understand what your business requires.

Do you need funding to get started?

Are you capable of starting and just using your business from day one without any investment? Or do you need money to get premises, supplies, marketing etc. carried out?

How much competition do you have?

Look around you both on the web and locally – who is potentially standing in your way and stopping you from being a success? Taking the time to understand this will help you become far more likely to succeed in the coming years. It's a small step, but a very important one.

As you can see, there are many questions to ask yourself about starting a business. To reach the height of your potential and to avoid limiting yourself to success, you should try and answer every question. Also, you have one more major factor to take into account that will vary depending on where you are based – registering your business.

Every country is different but you should make a point of speaking to an advisor or expert on this subject within your own country – they can help you understand where you might be going wrong.

Aside from this, your business needs to know its catchment area, the potential for success, the demand for your goods or services and the viability of being able to actually sell them. After all, your business has to make sense with both what people want and the kind of services or skills that you can provide!

There is no point starting a business with no demand or one that you cannot hope to actually provide the service for. Before you go any further, make sure that you can produce a logical and cohesive answer for everything that we just addressed. Next, we're going to take a look at various things that you would do well to consider if you want to have a chance of being a successful business.

Thank you and good luck!

Tom Mahalo

www.ingramcontent.com/pod-product-compliance
Lightning Source LLC
Chambersburg PA
CBHW070410190526
45169CB00003B/1193